MW01226023

FAM OUS GE RAN IUM

MICHELLE
MEIER

New York

ISBN: 978-0-9907154-1-2

FOR YOU

TABLE OF CONTENTS

ONE

TWO

THREE

ONE

ASHFIELD

It rained during the night,
a light rain.
I looked for something
to worry about but
there was nothing
only a towel I left out
slung over a garden chair.
The rest was far behind
or someone else's.
A spider's bite on the skin
produced a new limb
that was gone in the morning.
Or a spider's bite
did not appear on the skin
for close to a day
until the spider was
wound back up and
well hidden.
I knew things that appeared
at once lost and useful—
a rusted bolt in the grass,
the plot of another's dream.
Our lungs were bellows
and of all the flowers
that edged by our houses
and bridges only the scent
of the oldest roses
did we find unoffending.

COMMUNITY GARDEN

In the garden there are many birdhouse options
for the local birds. They may visit a mosque,
castle tower, barn, bait shop or
narrow Burgher's house,
its Flemish architectural details
likely lost on some neighborhood children
who are fighting. Their mothers warn
obliquely about the future.
TO ANYONE WHO IS SCREAMING
IT WILL BE TIME TO LEAVE.
A pair of pigeons enter via the cement stairs
along with two English speaking tourists
who agree this is a gem of a park
and remark they only have community
parking lots where they live.

THE RABBIT AND THE VANISHING POINT

The rabbit and the vanishing point are in love.
Fool's gold for eyes, plumes of ideas,
budding tonsils. Is this not love?
I like tapestries with the inclusion of
a Lamassu. At least two.
For protection. With apples, persimmons,
and elderflowers, too.
Thank you.
In the next room of the mind,
the room with less furniture,
objects are arranged in a curious way,
the outside brought inside.
A rose trellis above a chair.
A portrait of a lion.
Two magnets. Do magnets
only have a thought of the other?
Under the floorboards are rotting
eyelashes and other brambles
from the human body. The bakery across
the way is closed, full of day old bread
and closed levers. A woman runs the shop
and she is very beautiful.

LIST

I have no problem
committing to the unseen.
Rose lotion, underwear,
a feathered brush
to sweep up dust,
a cloth to clean the floors
and wash a few times,
throw out with coffee grinds
and dead parts of
angel plants and plastic
once fitted to the skin
of a fish I ate over
two days. There was
something I meant to do
but never made a list,
something I meant
to think about but never
made a list.

OF

Adeline of the salad,
Amelia of Bermuda,
Arabella of first love,
Valentine of the woolen glove,
Cole of the dog run,
Slim of the sea,
Phillipe of the lantern,
Leonard of Manhattan,
Serafina of the curtains,
Ingrid of the wood,
Jan of the grocery,
Solomon of the good,
Stephan of the sun,
Mae of the hunt,
Millicent of the house,
Fredrick of the arctic front,
Rosalyn of the sky,
Mina of the key,
Lucia of the dark,
Elsa of the tree,
Pearl of the public bus,
Clive of the elbow and also
of the knee.

STUDY #1

It would be dark
at night and this
left them in love.

NUMERATION

Three species of tree met
in the sky: alder, oak and fir
and in between, the sky
convalesced
through the spectral colors
of a bruise before the knee
and juncture of evening
would bend.

One species of framed flora
hung in a doctor's office:
an illustration of a turnip,
or was it something different,
windy, wildly shifting:
an anemone, a heliotrope?
Notably, it had a bulb
and root and Latin script below
too slight to see from where
I was seated.

A ghost entered in a suit
and tie and waited with me
until he was called into a room
where someone laughed.

The radio in the waiting room
played a medley of partial
symphonies to drown out a patient
and doctor's intimate talk.

QUESTION AT SIX A.M.

Somehow, I am awake and dressed
and available to watch a bird rest
improbably on a hanging, electrical
wire. Or is it so that no vertical or
horizontal surface is improbable for
birds, not even water?

SPEECH WITHOUT SPEECH

Speaking to someone else
without speech and to myself.
In the shower.
Over rice pudding at twilight.
Into the window sill between
winter and summer.
Up the hill and on a bench.
Through an archway.
To a satellite I never saw.
Mostly I spoke to you,
shoe to grass, the forest of nowhere
rushing past, and lingering
like a stranger at a gate,
someone who looked familiar
until it got dark.

STUDY #2

That whole evening
sullied and
quite pale and
so embarrassed.

VERSILIA

I changed beds during the night,
found myself closer to the window in the morning
and walking to the barn was a road
with many choices.
I thought, ravens still get sent ahead,
or of men moving backwards,
looking through a lens
or down the barrel of a gun.
The color blue was a place in Italy I used to go
where there was only future health
and a store below
that sold coffee and oil.
I had friends.
Were they friends as much as
would-be lovers?
Swimming naked I kept
rounding corners to make certain
they no longer think of me now.
The café, the monument,
the marble floors in the hall
and a train on a turn past a shy, old grove
strung up with smoke and pink oranges.

LARGER THAN THAT

Outside the Tuscan shack
there was a glass bowl
the size of a pumpkin,
filled with old water and
glittering fish.

Only it was larger—
the size of a chair—
like a chair placed on the table,
with an aquatic component.

Only it was larger than that,
a bathysphere,
its own watery castle,
descending through light
and time and landscape,
not of any fixed proportion
that could be explained
to the fish. I did not know
who fed them.

STUDY #9

The visitor traveled
out of his mind
by entering buildings
and five or six stories.

PACIFIC STREET

Yellow, a man thinks one morning over eggs
and hires a painter to paint the front door.
Reminds me of Tuscany, his neighbor says into
a cordless phone and looks down at her toes.
What is that red, the name of the flower
that was her mother's favorite?
Geraniums: The Complete Encyclopedia
lies open on a short wall with other paperbacks
about surgery or suicide. A woman takes them.
There are so many things she does not know
about herself.

RIP TIDES

There are two flags staked in the sand
and a friend says he thinks they mark
how high the tide rises.
No they don't, I say.
They mark where within
we are allowed to swim and still believe
that we'll be saved.
A woman asks a lifeguard:
Is there a rip tide today?
The same friend overhears
and says it's a silly question,
there are always rip tides.

GEOLOGICAL SURVEY

How old are you?
Looking at your response
in a little more detail
I see that you are just not speaking.
Here we arrive at two
important conclusions.
One: breakdown.
Two: the fact that stony
components of us have
moved to the outer part
of the mantel.
This is the anniversary of
how long we did not live.
In a new Stone Age,
about 7,000 years ago,
there were ash beds
and early artwork suggestive
of beauty or at the very least—
charcoal.

STUDY #3

Domed dream
of a carved bowl
poured
in the darkness.

CHILD DIVER

Tragedy of seemingly
disparate events—
piston, toffee,
all things sweetly wanting—
a lean child diving
with intent—
walk the board,
bounce once, project.

SEPTEMBER OF RETREAT

Fall: a lot of rot. It seems to start
at the tips of an otherwise
unremarkable tree but for its
blurred look and serifed names:
hemlock, hickory. Nearby,
a baby once awake, sleeps
and a pond seizes in an eerie moss.
The earth slips in the dark.
A season returns from the advance
of age. The forest is an envelope
of rude frogs.

THE APPLES

The apples fell
too early
and rotted.
Oh well.
This was what
occurred.

WHERE THE COWS LIVED

Not many people looked happy at the gym.
A woman rowed to nowhere,
asleep with her eyes open.
Some men assessed how to turn
the pull-down machine into a plough.
After, they went into the treadmill room
where the cows lived and required milking.
One man knelt like Atlas but looked
meek about it. Another knelt to pray.
I could not hear what he said, if he spoke
to God at all. What could I know.
No leaves blew in because of our glass case.
They scuttled around the base of us and
went still. This is how leaves sleep.

STORM

Bent lights. Burnt parts of a roof.
Dirt passages in corners of the garage.
Stepping on our own lace,
almost losing a shoe.
Leaves on a table. Leaves on a window.
Leaves on surfaces not the floor.
Suspiciously clean patios next door.
The sound of chewing—
the dishwasher.
No father has been around to order.
A propane tank left out in the storm.

THE OTHER SIDE

They stood close to the door.
They put an ear to it.
On the other side was an ailing balloon
drifting around the room.
It was dying.
It would take a few more days.

STUDY #15

To be clear about
clarity, by night
the pool whispered
back something
entirely inaudible.

TWO

IDEA

I start with a room and a voice.

The voice would like me to elaborate on my capacity for deprivation.

I'm allowed a pencil and paper and I draw a wood pile.
I don't know why.

After that, we discuss deprivation's relation to creation.

The room gets a table.

I ask the voice whom or what it would control with its mind if it could.
It stalls, then decides to answer honestly:

The voice has an ex-girlfriend.

The room gets a window.

It's winter and there's only the glow of a Northern sky and frozen snow.

I ask if it's a fact that we've all come from meteorites,
and the voice says it's possible,
it's read the latest issue of *Popular Science*
but there's no way to be sure.

I ask how long we'll be here, and the voice sounds tired, yawns,
thinks I mean cosmically, and maybe I do.

Says it's best if we continue in the morning.

I'm concerned I won't know the difference between now and morning,
but it drifts off and doesn't answer.

The sky dims. Stars.

Then the voice begins talking in its sleep about our Foreign Policy,
which, as I understand it from the voice, is crap.

I know how to stay quiet.

The room has a door now.

It's going so well.

I'll stay a little while longer.

A DREAM

A dream in which I lost a house
and much like fog
in the morning there was talk
amongst people about the
dramatic effect of its occurrence.

THE FAR AND NEAR

There's a crystal person sitting in
the crystal department of
the department store
like Father Time but a woman
who's a little younger but not by much.
She's always there.
She doesn't move.
She sits alone at night well after
security has shut off all the lights.
Rows of spot-lit champagne flutes
refract nothing spoken back.
Outside, the stars are a rim
of glass flowers
like a trellis prepared in the sky
for a marriage or birth, surgery
or funerary service. Inside, our brains
are brimming in the most translucent liquid
not yet found on other planets.

STUDY #5

Tomorrow
or the next day
a funeral;
storms of snow
and hail,
these weaker
branches.

SNOW IN THE NIGHT

It snowed in the night
and the parked cars changed
into strange potatoes.
Overhead in a plane
passengers ate small,
perfectly rendered carrots.
They fell asleep not reading
subtitles on screens,
not dreaming specifically,
of multiple moons,
a soft landing.
Or of a sudden test
in which they were asked
to quickly name
any song they loved,
or at the very least, liked,
and found, much to their own
dismay, they couldn't think
of even one.

COAT

The sable is not an animal of sermons.
Nor does it travel in a tribe.
How could such a little thing be nomadic?
In Siberia, the night's milky quartz
is filled with citrine roses.
The homes and shipping routes
of sables are China-mooned and
variegated. There's a difference between
working snow and just plain snow
or working rivers and just plain rivers.
The frozen stones are idlers.
This is the birch and arrowroot of
a love letter and also an old coat full
of sphinx moths.

STUDY #6

The polite madman
wrote them a receipt
for trembling.

DIAGNOSIS

In dreams when dissonant parts
of the past are stacked,
a hole is bored
to make a baby's game of drop
the round object in the round space.
Where is that, anyway?
Once I saw a seal atop a buoy
while passing it on a boat.
Underwater I found a dog
in a yard, crying at the bushes.

KENT

The stars cartwheeled down, etched their light
on the eyelids of sleepers.
We woke. Our houses vanished.
There was nothing else: not the job, or mail, or store,
no driveway leading out,
no discarded rakes or books.
There were no sounds.
There was the vague memory of window frames
and if we had been scared or sick
that it had happened, there was no undoing it.
Weeks later we would pause and envision this
as a place we had visited
as vast and collapsing as the whole galaxy.
Our beds had given way to grass.
Our waists were as thin as winter trees.
Then gently, one afternoon, the houses floated
back down, settling into their
old stone outlines.

OLD DREAMS

I rotated whole lagoons.
I goaled with a skull for a soccer ball.
The game never really got very far.
I hid under beds and made reports
to a police officer who arrived
too late.
My earrings were spared.
A lion claimed my right ankle.
I was tossed into the sky but eventually returned.
I slept in banks.
I was shot in the head.
When it stormed, the wind was too strong to weather,
and the rain was blue and stuck
to everything.

NEW TOOTH

Is it true the moon sheds?
Is it snow?

LANDSCAPE

The snow was the great leveler.
The cemetery's gates were an
art form weighted with
abstract flora. I could place a leaf
or stone below the wall if such
a thing were physically possible
given the weakness of my arms,
the invisibility of my resources.
Not even the wedges, inclines
and fulcrums that filled my home
were tangible. No telling when
they would materialize.

TALK

He talked himself into a hole.
It was made of lace.
He looked regretful after.
Where he ended was crocheted,
an old world technique.
He tried to backtrack but didn't know
the stitches to begin with.

AIRPORT HOTEL

My sister doesn't talk in her sleep, she whispers.
It's the closest we'll come to a relationship for now,
though once when we were both asleep
I finished her sentence.
You ask how I know this
and it is the same way
I am certain a brown cat broke through
the screen while I slept, leaden with jetlag.
There was a hole.
When we're awake, we're quieter,
until she makes a sound that I understand
to represent the entire soundtrack to *West Side Story*.
I can't stop laughing. Then I'm crying a little.
I'm tired. Then I don't see her again for
a long time. Do you want this piece of paper,
I say to her before leaving, because if you don't want it,
I'm going to put my gum in it. She doesn't want it.
I usually don't chew gum.

SOME DREAMS

Some dreams do not wake us
only hang there, a tilted
woodcut of a balcony
unable to speak or ask a
passing stranger for definition.

THE PORCELAIN ROOM

And there was peace, to be seated amongst unbroken objects.

Porcelain terrines, one hundred cups, a cherub, a tea pot,
lemons, a fleet of ships, a dragon, an island.

Everything was fixed, evenly lit, preserved, pristinely displayed,
silent and kept.

On the Cape, cascading trees and mossy crags resembled
green tiered cakes.

At a specific point on the path, fog was usually seen,
known to show itself in that one place.

Nearby a deer stood still, afraid or unafraid, haunted or only
looking haunted.

In a hotel room, stationery and an envelope on a desk.

From the window, the bright and vapid line of gray sea and sky
dotted with seal heads.

All night, cars spiraled down from a bridge and sparsely manned
boats from China passed under, coded and timed to a printed
paper log that appeared—to me—unreadable.

STUDY #14

Risen late
with the weight
of the usual.

PRIVATE SCHOOL ENTRY ROOM

Forces at work,
a chair pushing a rug
and the rug pushing back.
In photographs,
two teams for posterity.
Nine swimmers exposed for the century
above eight tennis players in sweaters.
The doormat, crooked
and encrusted with snow salt
displays the coat of arms,
a screaming lion
and a negative crescent
like the moon in shutters.
The bell remains quiet,
ruddy against green walls
the color of old gates,
but the secretary is expectant.
What a dreary day,
an entering man exclaims.

HOW

What to do with this pervasive sense of
the arbitrary? Winter is an onion or
a turnip. Or what's to keep me from
remembering a dogwood I once knew?
It expended its pink petals like coins.
The crickets resurrect in groups and hide
behind unbelievably narrow planes.
The swing's strings. How do they do this?

THREE WHITE PINE TREES

Within the edges of the week,
I use the same words until
the week elapses
and forget what they were,
remember I never
learned them.
There are crows awake behind
the house and a lake
traveling away.
Behind the next house,
sparrows and a man-made pool,
and the last house,
obsidian planted in the dirt
and strewn garbage bags
reflecting black. Often
I name places I've never been
Finland, and whole swaths of time,
night beyond description.
Bed in box, bed in bed, an accounting
of fixtures: a door, a table, a bench.
Three white pine trees in a field.

AS IT WANTED

It was so cold the baby turned into a hat.
The quarter machine at the Laundromat
gave three for every dollar.
The baby intuitively knew the injustice.
Ever since becoming a hat,
no one could see the baby's blinks
or breaths or if he breathed at all.
Some babies are very patient.

—

The snow arrived and marked the cruxes
of a tree. I set an alarm
and waited to be scared by its sound.
I don't have good news, I told myself.
The cat sprawled herself across
the kitchen table as if to endure a surgery.
Afterwards, she sat in the staging area
between two rooms.
The coffee was ground for its apotheosis.

—

What's another term for wire mesh?
I lost my English more than once.
It was too small to be mine.
I used my possessions any way they let me.
A tea cup for a ladle.
A white sheet for a large bag.
A necklace made of an unbroken
coil of orange rind.
A foot fell asleep—mine? I let it be
as it wanted.

A SHORT HISTORY

What's below this room if not the room below?
Where does the time not speaking go?
As if the mind was a cup of liquid spilled from
a table and draining quickly. Was I conscious
during the accident of this?

ORDINARILY INVISIBLE

In the museum, I took note of everything unexplained.
Stone objects of unknown use.
Figures not identified with any deity.
Glyphs inscribed on jade of uncertain meaning.
Mouths carved into a smirk or horse-shoe of sadness
and texts about shamans and their
occupational hazards.
I passed Berber nomads resting at blue nightfall,
and mirrors of iron, pyrite and marcasite,
serving as magical devices rather than as looking glasses.
The stars were underfoot and a canoe drifted in
the water of the sky.
I got lost looking for the giant slice of tree
and a docent told me to take a left
in the American Forests wing.
She drew a squiggle and a line on the floor plan to show,
inversely, which way to go
that looked like a yarn ball running away
from the dark string of itself.
Short count, long count,
past shells and minerals pressured into iridescence,
I found a cross section of a farmer's lawn,
partially titled *Ordinarily Invisible To Man*,
with a mole tunnel and a mole,
one earthworm and one toad.
When winter thawed, I left the farm,
and came upon an underground lair of wasps,
its shy and dangerous Queen, our mother, the foundress.
I went farther to the tree, striated coin of winds and history,
and mulled there quietly behind the tourists speaking
French and Portuguese.
I do not know what they said.
At home, I found a small, rose-glass mosaic tile
of unknown origins in the bathroom and concluded
it had fallen down from an unknown
shelf, off an unknown object of
unknown use, displayed just out of view,
some place else.

STUDY #7

Four o'clock
rested heavily
at each side street;
you could hear
a dull push.

BUT FOR

It was Sunday and quiet but for
the occasional child in the street.
The partial houses to those asleep
were framed with pillars,
columns and arcades,
with hallways leading down not out.
No oculus to the weather or
further intelligence
on the last meals of socialites,
or flute makers, fur traders,
horse race enthusiasts, magnates,
moguls, captains of industry,
died of a tumor, died of a question,
died of a surfeit of Turkish delight.
Gray out that day, but for asters
lying in wait and rust in full bloom
on the iron gates.

THE RAVISHING

The temperature
dropped
through a door
in the floor
and returned via
the chimney.
So many aspects
of longing
looped around
the house this way.

STUDY #10

Nothing until
nine o'clock
but then daybreak
went on for
a week or more.

THREE

THE BLUE BIRD

I felt this before I was embodied.
I went alone to the quarry.
I purchased a small piece of stone that opened.
I could hide the few jewels that I owned.
Once I lunched on a balcony.
Once I saw a woman swim from her home
because she could.
The lake was as deep as the mountains were high.
It held mirrored fish and thrown stems
from cherries.
I was a child again to a new mother.
I felt overwhelmed by this mother's accessories.
Glasses, earrings, necklace, headband,
too much together.
They interfered with the eyes,
the mouth, not removable except in
Gothic or Latin stories.

AFTER SHE DIED

After she died,
I saw a ghost wearing a red bow-tie
leaning against a tree.
Blackbirds raced into the sun.
A stained-glass cloud hung in the window pane.
It would be Halloween soon
and I understand people watch horror films
to feel frightened,
and I wonder about those people.
How is it that you are not already frightened?
In the middle of the night,
my friend and I rolled into my cigar box bed,
periodically talking and not talking.
What did she like? my friend asked,
and after a few minutes I said I didn't know
what she liked, only how she seemed.
It had been a long time,
she had stopped liking anything.
Sometimes I wandered in the small room
while my friend slept,
a long sleeper advancing.
The clock was not the clock.
It was the wind billowing into a flag
somewhere cold.
She asked me what I was thinking about
when she woke once and I said
Daniel Day Lewis,
and it was funny at this proximity to death
that I should be thinking
about an actor,
but I said it frightened me
how they leave into someone else,
how they could leave for a day or a week or a year,
and when they returned the answer
to where they had gone would be a name:
Abraham Lincoln.
And when I was in the shower, I told her,
and she had gone out for toilet paper,

I was frightened by the lack
of a third door—
burial, cremation and what else?
Ship? she suggested.
That's the same, I said.
It still burns and sinks or else
they shoot fire lit arrows at it until it does.
Back on the topic of actors, she considered,
it seems all this is about the unstable universe,
only she didn't use the word unstable,
and it wasn't chaotic,
and it wasn't illusory,
although she did use that word
at some point during the night.
I'm quite sure the word she used
to describe the universe began
with the letter P.
It's been one week
and still I can't think of it,
or else I never really knew it,
never heard her say it in first place.

STUDY #8

Demons, low ones,
rivers and forests
and grief,
not a foot of space
between the chairs.

CHILDREN PLAYING AT THE ALL-NIGHT LAUNDROMAT

The reflection in the small, still washer
is an eye, a convex vortex.
What's your name? one little girl says

to another, and not waiting for the answer
counts all the machines: one, two,
three until twelve, and laughs heartily into

the emptiness. Hello? she yells.
The other girl shows her how the doorknob
to the machine gets closed properly.

You turn it like this, do you see?

BY-NIGHT CRIME

At night the wind upsets the wooden railroad
of the house, upsets me too,
disorders a door, leaves through
an obvious hole on a bookshelf where a book
was not put back. Outside in the alley,
a false owl and red dust pan, its contents once
optical instruments, crushed and gathered
into dust, and sleep mounts like a wave
headed for a seaside town. There's a woman
at a café table whose toothbrush and wallet I,
for some reason, took.

I steal things in dreams.

TO THE CONCISE AND PRACTICED TRAVELER

Take care,
The mist may descend quickly.
You might find yourself without
a complete bathing outfit in
an ice storm that caused the rocks
to be so frozen.
Pay attention. Stay in bed.
Tell the doctor if you are
feeling giddy. If you need bandaging.
If you lose consciousness.

—

Mr., Mrs., Miss,
I wrote to you, did you not
receive my letter?

—

The concierge has your shoes
and this street does not lead
to the old town.

—

What is in this box?
Please help me close it,
I did not know I had to pay.

—

The beach is not where you thought.
Your luggage tickets were buried in the forum.
Should you like something sweet,
open the window and call for a porter.

—

There is no lift to the room
overlooking the sea
though you intend to stay
a week at least.

–

The hairdresser swerves.

–

It is half past six. It is ten to nine.
That bag is not mine and the
main spring of my watch is broken.

–

The eiderdown will give you allergies.
The switch by the staircase turns on
the light and hot water.

–

That cathedral has a secret ice-rink
and, at intervals, a tennis court.
That restaurant has a central waterfall.

–

The armchair was removed
and in its place is a lavender scarf
no one owns.

–

The basilica is interminably closed.

NORTHEAST

The light switches were coffins
and the brass knob
an eye of the room's only door.
Water boiled in a pot.
A candle rose and burned
the white wall gray.
Smoked, a past action or state.
Lilac, a color of the sky and
a piece of paper caught in the tree
of evening. The architecture
came and in between were farms
and cars and clergy.
They gathered in the grass
of the northeast and built
a cemetery here.

DOOR TO THE AFTERNOON

The key does not so much
open the lock
as it catches the door.
The floorboards descend more,
work to rest themselves further.
In the kitchen, the knife
will not give up the pit.
The summer's shadows
are hanging trophy rabbits.
A meal gets stewed and
served. The dead have stone
dining room tables and
their houses are owned by
at least two different churches.

STUDY #11

The oldest thought
had given them
a weighty subject.

BOOK DRAMA

The librarian on the second floor said
it was on the third floor and the librarian
on the third floor said it was on the second
floor or maybe in the basement.

It was an enormous disappointment.
As if the book were my new lover scheduled
to meet me at a predetermined corner
and never showed.

Found later in a quiet stack, I felt
a jolt of exhilaration that it had been
waiting all along and took it home
and didn't read it.

MIRROR

The body has different kinds of fat.
The folds of the skin resemble the ocean in a painting:
pink and frothed and changing constantly.
There's a new island.
It just showed up yesterday and I don't know
what I'll call it.
I saw it in the mirror, which is to say,
I saw it more than once.

THE BUG WHO LEFT THE LANDSCAPE

It didn't suit him.
He preferred a bedroom wall
in the suburbs.
He changed identities
by taking the form of a moth,
a house fly and,
at last, a lightening bug.
He could speak by turning off,
the longest intervals
of darkness were when
he shared himself
the most.

THE RIVER

Walking to the river I pass a woman reading in
the cemetery, seated in a low chair.
I would like a chair like hers for the cemetery,
for reading low like her. Reading, its own
succumbing to a plot. At the river, a boy lifts
his little brother up a lamppost, as if to permanently
attach him, a kind of boy finial. They strain
and strain. Their parents don't look on, which
seems to say the boys might achieve the height
they hope, so long as they are never caught.
This sort of venture between two brothers, one
helping the other to assume the form of an
inanimate object is a delicate business.
The river has a special feature. It tilts open like
a trunk. Inside are the fisherman, where they all go
on their days off. When they are not visibly fishing.

SHAME

It's the children who speak like adults
that surprise me the most. They say,
"Well, good for you!" or "Tell me, how is your life?"
and I am caught with long shoulders,
quite sure they can see how badly it has gone.

STUDY #12

Dinner amid
an unbroken line
of knives.

MUSEUM TOUR OF A POEM

The original form of
this poem is in ruins.
Parts of it were stolen
by archeologists or
thieves.
Its major structure is thought
to have been a doorway
made of limestone.
The original site of the doorway
is not known.
This is to say the poem
has no specific function except
to be walked through.
Inside, it houses medieval beasts,
both real and imagined,
and faceless clerics
as tombstone decoration.
In the next room,
there is an idealized King
missing his arms,
and with those gone,
the attribute he held in his hands,
signifying his identity.
I like to think
he held two glass stars,
both arms extended
to share the heavens with us
and his patrons.
I just made that up;
glass stars are not in any catalog
of common iconography
and, even if not a fiction,
would not survive intact
for this length of time.
Moving on,
this poem has a fountain
of an angry monster
that spits out cold water.

It also has a wooden box
depicting scenes of war
and unexpected love,
or turned and viewed another way,
scenes of capture and
of torture.
Its hallmarks of style are
the richness
of its motifs in contrast
with its plain surfaces.
At its center is a seated figure.
The architectonic function
of the figure is uncertain.
Nothing more is known
of its maker.
Outside, the poem has a cloister,
with lilac and daffodil patches
quivering in the wind
and sun as if
the world's turning
has been sped up,
and slowed in other senses.
Nearby there's a woman
asleep on a stone bench,
her head leaned against
a monastery wall, along which
cloaked monks
once disappeared in long strides
down the length of
its long hall.
The miracles of the poem
do not happen sequentially.
For eternity, there is
a carved hilt at the side
of its effigy of uncertain
cultural origin.
Many visitors, especially children,
like the serene look
of its closed eyes
and the lion on its coat of arms.

We have met our end
at its entrance. As I said,
the original form of this poem
was ruined and stolen
and is not known.

PROBLEMS AND IMPLICATIONS

In the final version of this day, we all played Boggle
and went home no worse for it. But that didn't
happen. In the first version, the men played
Chet Baker and smoked at the dining room table.
They were from Italy, there were no women,
I wasn't there. Nearby, in the dark, was a scalable
castle wall. In the fifty-first version, we searched
the streets and shops of the old city for sea-glass
bottles, for the translucent contours of them
to display on the mantles in our homes, all hues,
though we comprehended the problems and implications
of this sort of collecting behavior.

SICILY

Something about the top of a shoe,
the cut of a sock. A man on a train
watches me not read my book.
He watches the tunnel of my thoughts.
It's all Fascist seaside infrastructure,
a long turn into the dark and
back out. It won't hold. Eventually,
the tunnel will exist in a crumble
on the ocean's lowest register.
I was having an idea. That sunlight
must be searched for like something
truly rare to parse out. A window
turns into a chandelier and into a
stalactite. That was all I had. That
was all I saw. That was the film's entire
plot so far.

EPISODES

Some days I can't tell the difference
between dogwoods or deep sea fish.
Nor can I account for stories hidden
in window glass or the insect paused
to read them. The cranberry color
of certain spring flowers is deceptive,
acts like a departed relative—
pervasive, fragrant. Surrounding
clouds pose in ways that denote prayer
before disappearing altogether.
So goes the sensation of heat or cold
or dreams that harpoon into the side
of the head. The air is jeweled and
nervous. As seen from far away,
both the water and sky behave much
like quartz. The elms drop their keys
and sermons and leave without
closing the garden gate. It is May.
It is late. At night, the moon is renovated
and landscaped to look like a real place
where human problems are examined
as if under magnification.

PARTS OF LEAVES

On a form,
in the space for my name,
I write "intermittent."
On the train,
a woman's eyes
are made of oysters.
Some sleeves are
actually for
the neck,
a delicate place different
from a drugstore.
All week,
the kitchen cabinets
disassemble themselves,
wood shard by
wood shard
until they are destitute
and not even there.
The weather turns warmer.
Parts of leaves emerge
but are yet to be invented.

SPRING IS HERE

Once green, the graves were
luminous again but I harbored
superstition about the stone
maiden with no head and why
the daffodils are always first.

TWO SENSES

On Friday, I loitered in an unfurnished room,
dropped medicine in an animal's eye,
not her ear, a tunnel to I don't know where.
Like cells in a dish suddenly macroscopic,
outside a spruce tree and doorman-philosopher,
with a circle of keys and rolling closet,
balconies of stars and an accordion player
singing a bilingual tune about depression—

I stared at him to hear it better—

STUDY #13

Such were
the evening
and a bird
only their misery
to talk of.

GIANT RABBIT

Mining myself for something
I believe to be
in the ballpark of the truth,
I think the tree outside
my window at night
looks like a giant golden rabbit:
feral, illuminated,
but usually hidden from
plain sight in the daytime.

PROGNOSIS

The curtains want the wind in them.
They swell open in slow motion.
Some days the sun is so bright it's like
a storm. Our eyes adjust and

it is warming; we are warmed.
Of this room, these curtains,
are they technically touching? So far
they are not. They balloon around

the other's edges. Gulped, the way
the apple of the throat moves inside
of nervousness. So, do they ever kiss?
Yes. The same way planets crash

into each other and cease to exist
but become something else.
Very slowly and very far in the future.
So far from now the end appears blurry
and very soft.

STUDY #14

An interpreter
was found
beneath the fields.

AFTERWORD

It is important to be receptive to finding the beautiful stories in your life.

My spouse and I had recently laid his father to rest after a long and terrible illness, and I was recovering from a painful malady. It was the start of spring, which heralded some kind of change from the past six months of a hard, sad autumn and winter.

A dear college friend, Heather Klinkhamer, contacted me about an intriguing event at New York City's Rubin Museum, which specializes in art of the Asian Himalayas. It was hosting a Dreamover. This entailed bringing a sleeping bag in which to sleep overnight under an assigned artwork in the museum. A psychotherapist would wake us around 6 a.m. to record our dreams and see if they had any relevance with the artwork. Each participant was assigned a personal docent who guided us to our artwork, helped set up our beds, and engaged us in a discussion about our assigned art. Before we went to sleep, our personal docent read us a "goodnight story" related to our artwork to prime the dream pumps prior to slumber.

It felt extremely awkward to be read to by a stranger while I was lying down—I had to resist bolting up to be at eye level—but as my docent continued to read, my tension dissipated, and I became aware of the poem she was reading. When she finished, I inquired about the origin of the poem, *Episodes* (page 88), imagining that it was translated from 12th-century Burmese, since it was obviously relevant to the tiny Burmese stele I was sleeping under. I was flabbergasted to learn that the docent, Michelle Meier, had written this poem herself! I gave her my card and encouraged her to contact me with more of her work.

From a random meeting at a random event in a city of more than eight million people, I connected with Michelle Meier, and we proudly present her *Famous Geranium*, a book of exquisite poems. We hope this volume has enriched your life as much as the genesis of its happenstance did for us.

Karyn Kloumann
Founder and Publisher, Nauset Press
January 2015

ADDENDUM

"Whether it was the following Sunday when I saw the gentleman again, or whether there was any greater lapse of time before he reappeared, I cannot recall. I don't profess to be clear about dates. But there he was, in church, and he walked home with us afterwards. He came in, too, to look at the famous geranium we had, in the parlor-window. It did not appear to me that he took much notice of it, but before he went he asked my mother to give him a bit of the blossom. She begged him to choose it for himself, but he refused to do that—I could not understand why—so she plucked it for him, and gave it into his hand. He said he would never, never part with it any more; and I thought he must be quite a fool not to know that it would fall to pieces in a day or two."

—Charles Dickens, *David Copperfield*

ACKNOWLEDGEMENTS

Grateful acknowledgement is made to the editors of *POOL Poetry*, in which earlier versions of "How," "Problems and Implications," and "Snow in the Night," first appeared.

"To the Concise and Practiced Traveler" is drawn from a 1968 reprint of a *Collin's Italian Phrase Book: Clear and Concise for Travellers Abroad*, copyright William, Collins, Sons & Co., Ltd., London and Glasgow, 1963.

"Book Drama" is for Kate Hanna and Anne Bitsch.

With love and thanks to my friends, particularly Ella Brians, Sherisse Alvarez and Miranda Field for their discernment and advice during the shaping of this work while in manuscript.

Many thanks to Karyn Kloumann, Iris Sutcliffe, Marta López-Luaces and Geoffrey Nutter for their support and kind words.

ABOUT THE AUTHOR

Michelle Meier lives in Washington Heights, NY. This is her first collection of poems.

Made in the USA
Middletown, DE
15 May 2015